The Entrepreneur's Blueprint: Building a Business and Mastering Business Credit

Kay Thomas

Table of Contents:

Chapter 1: Introduction to Entrepreneurship

Chapter 2: Choosing the Right Business Structure

Chapter 3: Creating a Solid Business Plan

Chapter 4: Financial Management and Budgeting

- Creating a realistic budget and accounting for startup costs

- Understanding the importance of financial projections and cash flow management

Chapter 5: Building Business Credit

- Explaining what business credit is and why it's important

- Discussing the factors that contribute to a business credit score

- Strategies for building and improving business credit from scratch

-What are the exact steps for building business credit:

-Your foolproof plan to obtaining thousands in business credit

-Tiered business credit accounts

Chapter 6: Establishing a Strong Business Presence

-How to create a website, phone number and business address for your business

- Creating a professional brand identity and online presence

- Using effective marketing and networking strategies to attract customers

- Leveraging social media and other platforms to promote the business

Chapter 7: Legal and Regulatory Considerations

- Navigating the legal and regulatory requirements for starting a business

- Understanding tax obligations, licenses, permits, and other legal considerations

- Protecting the business through appropriate insurance and risk management

-Explain tax obligations of different business structures

Chapter 8: Securing Funding and Financing Options

- Exploring different sources of business funding (loans, investors, crowdfunding, etc.)

- Understanding the pros and cons of each funding option

- Tips for securing financing for a new business and managing financial resources effectively

-Marketing for your business

Chapter 9: Managing Growth and Scaling the Business

- Strategies for scaling the business while maintaining financial stability

- Managing expansion, hiring employees, and building a strong team

- Understanding the challenges and opportunities of business growth

Chapter 10: Navigating Pitfalls and Ensuring Long-Term Success

- Identifying common pitfalls and challenges faced by new business owners

- Tips for overcoming obstacles and adapting to changes in the business landscape

- Planning for long-term success and sustainability in the competitive business world

Glossary

References

About the Author:

Radiographer

Business owner

Published author

Homeschooling mother of 2

Beyond my literary pursuits, I am a driven business owner who has turned my passion for health and wellness into a thriving entrepreneurial endeavor. I started a Publishing company to encourage the youth to learn about topics not typically focused on in the public schooling system. Through my literary works, I promote financial literacy to the youth.

In my professional career, I am a skilled radiographer who brings compassion and expertise to my work in the medical field. My commitment to providing exceptional care to my patients is evident in my approach to my work, and I am deeply respected by my friends and colleagues for my dedication and professionalism.

One of my core values is a deep commitment to health and wellness, which I incorporate into every aspect of my life. As a plant-based eater, I believe in the power of nourishing the body with whole, natural foods, and I am passionate about sharing my insights and experiences with others who are on a similar wellness journey. My dedication to living a healthy lifestyle has a profound impact on my family and social media community, inspiring others to prioritize their well-being and make positive choices for their health.

In my free time, I enjoy immersing myself in nature, practicing yoga, and exploring new ways to incorporate mindfulness into my daily routine. I understand the importance of self-care and make it a priority to recharge and rejuvenate, allowing me to continue to thrive in both my personal and professional endeavors.

Overall, I strive to be a remarkable individual who exemplifies the values of dedication, compassion, and resilience. My multifaceted roles as a homeschooling mom, author, business owner, and radiographer showcase my unwavering commitment to making a positive impact in the lives of those around me. I advocate for holistic education,mindful wellness and I emphasize to people the power of acting on your dreams and desires. I hope to be an inspiration to others, empowering them to lead fulfilling and purpose-driven lives.

Introduction:

Welcome to "The Entrepreneur's Blueprint," a definitive guide to navigating the intricate journey of building a successful business and mastering the art of business credit. Whether you are a budding entrepreneur with a groundbreaking idea or an established business owner seeking to scale your enterprise, this book will equip you with the knowledge and strategies essential for sustainable growth and financial stability.

The path to business ownership is rife with challenges and uncertainties, yet it is also brimming with opportunities for innovation, impact, and success. In this book, we delve into the fundamental principles of entrepreneurship, from conceptualizing your business idea and crafting a robust business plan to securing funding and navigating the complexities of building a solid business credit profile.

Building a business goes beyond mere transactions and profits; it is a testament to resilience, creativity, and unwavering determination. We explore the crucial elements of developing a compelling brand identity, understanding your target audience, and crafting effective marketing strategies to propel your business into the global marketplace.

In the realm of business credit, we uncover the intricacies of establishing and nurturing a strong credit profile for your business. From demystifying the process of building business credit to decoding the avenues for financing, we arm you with the tools necessary to cultivate financial credibility, access capital, and forge enduring partnerships with suppliers and lenders.

Through real-world examples, actionable insights, and expert guidance, "The Entrepreneur's Blueprint" is designed to be a trusted companion on your entrepreneurial journey, offering invaluable wisdom to overcome challenges, capitalize on opportunities, and chart the course for long-term success.

Whether you are venturing into the world of entrepreneurship for the first time or seeking to fortify your existing business, this book is a testament to the unwavering spirit of innovation and the transformative power of strategic acumen. As we embark on this transformative exploration of business-building and credit mastery, may you be inspired, empowered, and fortified with the knowledge to turn your business aspirations into enduring realities.

Here is a fictional story illustrating your potential:
In a bustling city, there was a determined entrepreneur named Sarah. Sarah had always dreamt of creating her own business, and after years of gaining experience in the corporate world,

she decided to pursue her passion for organic skincare products. With unwavering determination and a clear vision, she embarked on the journey of building her own business from the ground up.

Sarah's first step was to meticulously research the market, identify potential customers, and understand their skincare needs. She spent countless hours studying the properties of natural ingredients and formulating products that would be both effective and gentle on the skin. Through dedication and perseverance, she honed her craft and developed a unique line of organic skincare solutions that she believed in wholeheartedly.

Armed with her product line and a solid business plan, Sarah sought guidance from a mentor who had experience in the beauty industry. With the mentor's support, she refined her business strategy, outlined her sales and marketing approach, and crafted a compelling brand story that showcased her commitment to quality and sustainability.

After carefully considering her options, Sarah decided to establish her business as a limited liability company (LLC) to protect her personal assets and gain credibility with potential partners and customers. She also secured a business address in a vibrant neighborhood and set up a professional website to showcase her products and engage with customers online. Additionally, she obtained a business phone number to provide excellent customer service and to separate her business communications from personal calls.

As she delved into the world of entrepreneurship, Sarah embraced the importance of building strong financial foundations for her business. She acquired a business credit account and diligently managed her company's cash flow, ensuring that she maintained a healthy balance between revenue and expenses. She also sought out small business loans to fund initial production and marketing efforts, allowing her to bring her products to market.

With her meticulously crafted business plan and a clear understanding of her target market, Sarah launched her organic skincare line with a small but impactful event, inviting local influencers and beauty bloggers to experience her products firsthand. This sparked interest and positive reviews, leading to an increase in sales and the gradual growth of her customer base.

Sarah's dedication and unwavering commitment to quality and sustainability began to pay off as her business gained traction. She built strong relationships with suppliers who shared her values, and she found like-minded individuals who were passionate about the natural beauty movement. She expanded her product line and formed partnerships with local spas and wellness centers, further establishing her brand in the market.

Despite the inevitable challenges and setbacks along the way, Sarah remained resilient and adaptable, constantly refining her business strategies and seeking feedback from her customers. Her hard work and perseverance paid off, and her business continued to flourish, gaining recognition for its commitment to ethical production practices and high-quality, eco-friendly skincare products.

As time passed, Sarah's business grew from a small startup to a thriving company with a loyal customer base and a positive impact on the community. She found fulfillment in knowing that she was creating products that improved people's lives while staying true to her vision of promoting natural beauty and sustainability.

In the end, Sarah's journey from a budding entrepreneur to a successful business owner was a testament to her unwavering passion, her willingness to learn and adapt, and her commitment to creating a business that aligned with her values. Her story inspired others to pursue their entrepreneurial dreams, showing that with dedication and perseverance, even the most ambitious business ventures can come to fruition. Everyone is capable of being just like Sarah or even going beyond.

Chapter 1: Introduction to Entrepreneurship and Business Credit

"The only way to do great work is to love what you do." - Steve Jobs

As you embark on the journey of entrepreneurship, it's essential to understand the fundamental principles that underpin successful ventures. This chapter serves as an introduction to the dynamic world of entrepreneurship, emphasizing the critical role of business credit in shaping the trajectory of new ventures.

Defining Entrepreneurship:
Entrepreneurship encapsulates the spirit of innovation, resilience, and vision. It represents the driving force behind transformative ideas, propelling them from mere concepts to thriving businesses. At its core, entrepreneurship is about identifying opportunities, taking calculated risks, and creating value in the marketplace. Throughout history, entrepreneurs have played a pivotal role in shaping economies, driving progress, and revolutionizing industries. Understanding the essence of entrepreneurship lays a strong foundation for aspiring business owners.

Qualities of Successful Entrepreneurs:
Successful entrepreneurs exhibit a distinct set of
qualities that contribute to their triumphs. These
include unwavering determination, adaptability,
creativity, and a penchant for calculated risk-taking.
The ability to persevere in the face of challenges,
innovate in rapidly evolving landscapes, and inspire
others with a compelling vision are hallmark traits of
impactful entrepreneurs. By delving into these
defining characteristics, aspiring business owners
can cultivate a mindset aligned with success and
sustainability.

Entrepreneurs possess a diverse set of
characteristics that contribute to their success in
creating and growing businesses. Some key traits
of successful entrepreneurs include:

- **Visionary Leadership:** Entrepreneurs
  often have a clear vision for their business
  and the ability to inspire and motivate others
  to share in that vision. They are
  forward-thinkers who can anticipate market
  trends and opportunities.

- **Passion and Determination:**
  Entrepreneurs are driven by a strong
  passion for their ideas and a relentless
  determination to see them come to fruition.
  They are willing to invest time, effort, and
  resources to overcome obstacles and
  challenges.

- **Risk-Taking Propensity:** Entrepreneurs
  are comfortable with taking calculated risks
  and making bold decisions to propel their
  businesses forward. They understand that
  risk is inherent in innovation and growth.

- **Adaptability:** Successful entrepreneurs
  are adaptable and open to change. They
  can pivot their strategies based on market
  feedback and evolving business
  landscapes.

- **Resilience:** Entrepreneurs often face
  setbacks and failures, but their resilience
  allows them to bounce back, learn from their
  experiences, and continue pursuing their
  goals.

- **Creativity and Innovation:** Entrepreneurs
  are often innovative thinkers who can
  identify novel solutions to existing problems
  or create entirely new products or services.

- **Strong Work Ethic:** Entrepreneurs are
  known for their work ethic, often putting in
  long hours and hard work to build and grow
  their businesses.

- **Customer-Centric Mindset:** Successful
  entrepreneurs prioritize understanding and
  meeting the needs of their customers,

building products or services that add value to their customers' lives.

- **Networking and Relationship Building:** Entrepreneurs understand the value of building strong networks and relationships, whether with potential partners, investors, or customers, to support their business growth.

- **Financial Acumen:** Entrepreneurial success often involves sound financial management, including budgeting, forecasting, and prudent investment decisions.

These characteristics, when combined, create a comprehensive profile of an entrepreneur who is poised to navigate the challenges, seize opportunities, and drive the success of their ventures.

Exploring the Mindset and Skills Needed to Start a Business:
Starting a business demands more than just a novel idea; it necessitates a unique mindset and a diverse skill set. Entrepreneurs must possess an entrepreneurial mindset characterized by agility, problem-solving acumen, and a relentless pursuit of improvement. In addition, foundational skills such as strategic planning, financial literacy, leadership, and effective communication play instrumental roles in navigating the complexities of business

ownership. By recognizing and honing these attributes, individuals can better equip themselves for the rigors of entrepreneurship.

What do you need to start a business:
To start a business, several key elements and considerations are essential to lay a strong foundation for success:

- **Business Idea**: Every successful business starts with a clear and compelling business idea. This idea should address a specific need or solve a problem in the market. Conducting thorough market research to validate the idea's viability and demand is crucial.

- **Business Plan**: Developing a comprehensive business plan that outlines the mission, vision, goals, target market, products or services, marketing and sales strategies, operational plan, and financial projections is vital. A well-crafted business plan serves as a roadmap for the business's direction and helps in securing financing.

- **Legal Structure:** Deciding on the legal structure of the business, such as a sole proprietorship, partnership, limited liability company (LLC), or corporation is important. Each structure has distinct legal and tax implications, and the choice should align with the business's goals and risk management needs.

- **Business Name and Registration:** Selecting a business name that reflects the brand and resonates with the target audience is crucial. Registering the business name and obtaining the necessary licenses and permits from local and state authorities are essential steps.

- **Funding:** Determining the financial requirements to start and sustain the business and exploring funding options such as personal savings, small business loans, venture capital, or angel investors is necessary. A clear understanding of the financial needs and available resources is critical for successful business launch and operations.

- **Business Location:** Depending on the nature of the business, selecting a suitable location, whether physical or virtual, is important. Considerations such as proximity to target customers, access to suppliers, and zoning regulations should be factored in.

- **Business Branding:** Developing a strong brand identity, including a logo, brand colors, and visual elements that convey the business's personality and values, is crucial. Establishing a professional and consistent brand presence is essential for customer recognition and loyalty.

- **Technology and Infrastructure:** Setting up the necessary technological infrastructure, such as communication systems, digital platforms, and operational tools, to support business operations and customer interactions is vital.

- **Legal and Regulatory Compliance:** Understanding the legal and regulatory requirements specific to the industry and location where the business operates is crucial. Compliance with tax laws, employment regulations, and business permits is essential for avoiding legal issues.

- **Team and Talent:** Planning for human resource needs and building a competent team with diverse skills and expertise is important. Hiring the right talent or identifying partners and advisors who complement the business's objectives can contribute to its success.

- **Marketing and Sales Strategy:** Developing a robust marketing and sales strategy to generate awareness, attract customers, and drive revenue is essential. This includes defining the target audience, identifying competitive advantages, and selecting appropriate marketing channels.

By addressing these foundational elements and considerations, aspiring entrepreneurs can lay a strong groundwork for launching and building a successful business. Each aspect plays a critical role in shaping the business's trajectory and fostering sustainable growth.

Importance of Understanding Business Credit: Amidst the myriad considerations of launching a new venture, the impact of business credit often stands as a cornerstone element. A firm grasp of business credit can significantly influence the trajectory of a new business, shaping its access to capital, vendor relationships, and overall financial health. It serves as a metric of trust and reliability, often influencing partnerships and opportunities for expansion. Understanding the nuances of business credit empowers entrepreneurs to make informed financial decisions, establish solid foundations for growth, and mitigate risks associated with leveraging credit.

The convergence of entrepreneurship and business credit underscores the interconnected nature of launching and scaling a successful venture. By delving into the essential elements of entrepreneurship and recognizing the pivotal role of business credit, aspiring business owners can lay the groundwork for sustainable, impactful, and resilient enterprises.

Chapter 2: Choosing the Right Business Structure

"Success is not the key to happiness. Happiness is the key to success. If you love what you are doing, you will be successful." - Albert Schweitzer

Selecting the appropriate business structure is a critical decision that significantly impacts the operations, legal standing, and financial outcomes of a new venture. This chapter delves into the intricacies of different business structures, guiding entrepreneurs in identifying the most suitable option based on their unique goals and circumstances. By exploring the legal and financial implications of each structure, prospective business owners can make informed choices aligned with their vision for the business.

Comparing Various Business Structures:
Entrepreneurs embarking on the path of business ownership are confronted with a spectrum of structures to choose from, each with distinct characteristics and implications. Sole proprietorship, partnership, limited liability company (LLC), corporation, and cooperative stand as prominent options, each offering a unique blend of liability, tax considerations, management flexibility, and regulatory obligations. By comparing and

contrasting these structures, individuals gain a comprehensive understanding of the framework within which their business will operate, enabling them to make decisions in line with their strategic objectives and risk tolerance. There are several business structures available, and each has its own characteristics, advantages, and disadvantages. The choice of business structure depends on various factors, including the nature of the business, ownership preferences, liability considerations, tax implications, and regulatory requirements. Here are the common types of business structures:

1. **Sole Proprietorship**:
   - Owned and operated by a single individual.
   - Simple and cost-effective to establish and maintain.
   - The owner has full control over business decisions.
   - The owner is personally liable for business debts and obligations.

2. **Partnership**:
   - Formed by two or more individuals sharing ownership and management responsibilities.
   - Partners share profits, losses, and liabilities according to a partnership agreement.
   - Can be a general partnership or a limited partnership, offering different levels of liability protection.

3. **Limited Liability Company (LLC):**
   - Blends elements of a partnership and a corporation.
   - Offers limited liability protection for owners, shielding personal assets from business liabilities.
   - Provides flexibility in management structure and tax treatment.
   - Requires less formalities compared to a corporation but offers similar liability protection.

4. **Corporation:**
   - A separate legal entity distinct from its owners (shareholders).
   - Provides limited liability protection to shareholders, allowing them to safeguard personal assets from business debts and liabilities.
   - Offers flexibility in ownership and transfer of shares.
   - Can be structured as a C corporation or an S corporation, each with different tax implications.

5. **S Corporation:**
   - Offers the limited liability protection of a corporation while avoiding double taxation.
   - Income, deductions, and credits flow through to the shareholders' personal tax returns.
   - Has specific eligibility requirements and must adhere to certain operational guidelines to maintain S corporation status.

6. **Nonprofit Organization:**

- Operates for charitable, educational, religious, or scientific purposes.
- Exempt from federal income taxes and may be eligible for various benefits and grants.
- Governed by a board of directors or trustees and operates for the benefit of the public or specific causes.

7. **Cooperative (Co-op):**
- Owned and operated by its members, who share in the profits and benefits according to their participation.
- Members have an equal say in the decision-making process, typically operating democratically.
- Often found in agriculture, consumer, and worker cooperatives.

Choosing the most suitable business structure is a critical decision for entrepreneurs, as it impacts aspects such as taxation, liability, management, and operational requirements. It's advisable to seek guidance from legal, financial, and tax professionals when evaluating the best structure for a new or existing business. Business owners should consider the long-term implications of their choice and ensure that the selected structure aligns with their business goals and operational needs.

Identifying the Best Structure for the New Business:

The optimal business structure for a new venture hinges upon the owner's specific aspirations, risk appetite, and long-term objectives. Sole proprietorship, for instance, offers simplicity and full control but entails unlimited personal liability. Conversely, a limited liability company provides liability protection and tax flexibility while demanding administrative formalities. Partnerships foster collaboration but require clear agreements and shared responsibilities. Understanding these distinctions equips entrepreneurs to align their business structure with their overarching vision, risk tolerance, and growth trajectory.

Exploring the Legal and Financial Implications: Each business structure carries a distinct set of legal and financial implications that directly influence the business's compliance requirements, tax liabilities, and financial arrangements. Sole proprietorships and partnerships afford simplicity but intertwine personal and business finances, while corporations and LLCs delineate business and personal assets, providing liability protection. Tax considerations, such as pass-through taxation in partnerships and S corporations, amplify the complexity of decision-making. By delving into these legal and financial ramifications, entrepreneurs can proactively position their businesses for regulatory adherence, financial stability, and long-term viability.

The process of choosing the right business structure requires a comprehensive understanding of the nuanced implications of each option. By weighing the legal, financial, and operational aspects of various structures and aligning them with their specific goals and circumstances, aspiring business owners can embark on their entrepreneurial endeavors with a solid foundation tailored to their vision, risk tolerance, and growth trajectory.

Chapter 3: Creating a Solid Business Plan

"Your work is going to fill a large part of your life, and the only way to be truly satisfied is to do what you believe is great work. And the only way to do great work is to love what you do." - Steve Jobs

Crafting a robust business plan is a fundamental step in the journey of establishing a successful venture. This chapter illuminates the significance of a well-structured business plan, guiding entrepreneurs through the process of researching and analyzing the market, competition, and target audience, ultimately enabling them to develop a comprehensive plan in alignment with their business goals and vision.

Understanding the Purpose and Components of a Business Plan:
A compelling business plan serves as a roadmap that outlines the business's mission, vision, goals, and the strategies to achieve them. It encompasses key components such as an executive summary, company description, market analysis, organization and management structure, product or service line, marketing and sales strategies, funding requirements, and financial projections. Understanding the purpose of each section

empowers entrepreneurs to communicate their business concept effectively, setting a clear direction for stakeholders and potential investors while guiding internal operations.

Creating a business plan is a fundamental step for entrepreneurs seeking to establish a new business or expand an existing one. A well-crafted business plan serves as a roadmap for the business, outlining its mission, vision, goals, strategies, and financial projections. Here are the key steps to create a comprehensive business plan:

1. **Executive Summary:**
   - Begin with a concise overview of the business, its purpose, and the problem it aims to solve.
   - Include key highlights such as the unique value proposition, target market, and financial projections.

2. **Company Description:**
   - Provide detailed information about the business, including its history, mission, vision, and the products or services offered.
   - Describe the business's industry, target market, and the competitive landscape.

3. **Market Analysis**:
   - Conduct thorough research to understand the target market, industry trends, customer needs, and the behavior of competitors.
   - Identify the business's competitive advantages and market positioning.

4. Organization and Management:

- Detail the organizational structure of the business, including the management team, key personnel, and their roles and responsibilities.
- Highlight the professional backgrounds and relevant experience of the leadership team.

5. Products or Services:

- Describe the specific products or services offered by the business, including their features, benefits, and unique selling points.
- Explain how the offerings fulfill customer needs and differentiate from those of competitors.

6. Marketing and Sales Strategy:

- Outline the marketing and sales approach, including market positioning, pricing strategy, promotional tactics, and sales channels.
- Specify the target demographics, customer acquisition strategies, and plans for customer retention.

7. Financial Projections:

- Develop detailed financial forecasts, including income statements, cash flow projections, and balance sheets for the first few years of operation.
- Include key financial metrics such as break-even analysis, return on investment, and sales forecasts.

8. Funding Request (If Applicable):

- If seeking funding, clearly articulate the capital requirements, the purpose of the funding, and the potential sources of financing.

- Provide an overview of the business's funding history, if applicable, and the proposed terms of the investment or loan.

9. **Appendix:**

- Include any supplementary information, such as resumes of key team members, market research data, legal documents, and any other relevant material.

It's crucial to tailor the business plan to the specific needs and context of the business, ensuring that it accurately reflects the business's goals, strategies, and unique value proposition. The plan should be realistic, well-researched, and supported by data and analysis. Additionally, it's important to review and update the business plan regularly to reflect changes in the market, industry, or business operations. A well-prepared business plan can instill confidence in potential investors, lenders, and stakeholders and serve as a guiding document for the business's growth and development.

How to Research and Analyze the Market, Competition, and Target Audience:
Thorough market research is imperative for identifying opportunities and challenges in the business landscape. Analyzing market trends, consumer behavior, and industry dynamics

provides invaluable insights into demand patterns, competitive forces, and potential strategies for market penetration. In addition, a detailed assessment of the competition unveils existing gaps, benchmarks, and best practices, guiding the formulation of a unique value proposition. Understanding the target audience, including their preferences, pain points, and consumption habits, facilitates the customization of products, services, and marketing approaches to resonate with the market segment effectively.

Developing a Comprehensive Business Plan Aligned with Goals and Vision:
Integrating the findings from market research and competition analysis, entrepreneurs can develop a comprehensive business plan that aligns with their specific goals and vision. By articulating a clear mission statement and delineating achievable short-term and long-term objectives, the plan sets the trajectory for sustainable growth and success. Communicating an in-depth understanding of the market, competition, and target audience within the plan portrays a well-informed and strategic approach to stakeholders, instilling confidence in the viability and potential of the business concept.

Entrepreneurs can also integrate operational and financial strategies within the plan to demonstrate the internal mechanisms that support the execution of the business model. This includes outlining organizational structure, operational processes, sales and marketing tactics, and realistic financial projections. Presenting a well-defined business plan not only serves as a guiding document for the founding team but also becomes a powerful tool for attracting investment, securing loans, or engaging potential partners who can contribute to the business's growth and success.

In essence, the process of creating a solid business plan encompasses a holistic understanding of the market, competition, and target audience, enabling entrepreneurs to articulate a strategic roadmap that harmonizes with their business goals and vision. Thorough research, meticulous analysis, and strategic formulation culminate in a comprehensive plan that not only captivates stakeholders but also serves as a dynamic blueprint for navigating the complexities of the business landscape and achieving sustainable growth.

Chapter 4: Financial Management and Budgeting

"The secret of change is to focus all your energy not on fighting the old, but on building the new." - Socrates

Establishing effective financial management and budgeting practices is pivotal for the success and sustainability of any business endeavor. This chapter delves into the essential elements of financial management, guiding entrepreneurs through the process of setting up financial systems, creating realistic budgets, accounting for startup costs, and understanding the significance of financial projections and cash flow management.

Setting up Financial Systems and Tools for Managing Business Finances:
Implementing robust financial systems and tools is fundamental for maintaining transparency, accuracy, and control over the business's monetary transactions. Entrepreneurs should explore and select appropriate accounting software, invoicing platforms, and financial management tools that align with the specific needs and scale of their business. Furthermore, establishing clear processes for tracking income, expenses, invoicing,

and financial reporting fosters efficiency and enables informed decision-making. This may involve appointing or outsourcing financial professionals to manage financial operations and ensure compliance with regulatory requirements.

Creating a Realistic Budget and Accounting for Startup Costs:
Developing a comprehensive and realistic budget is essential for prudent financial management. Entrepreneurs, anticipating both one-time startup costs and ongoing operational expenses, must meticulously outline all potential expenditures across various categories, including but not limited to, equipment, technology, marketing, personnel, and overheads. By factoring in contingencies and unforeseen expenses, business owners can mitigate financial risks and lay a sturdy foundation for financial stability. Additionally, accurate forecasting of initial capital requirements and diligent allocation of funds within the budget plan facilitate informed decision-making and prudent resource utilization during the critical early stages of the business.Securing funding for a startup business can be achieved through various avenues, each with its own set of requirements and considerations. Here are several common methods for obtaining funding for a startup:

1. **Self-Funding:**

- Use personal savings, assets, or other personal resources to finance the initial stages of the business.

- Consider tapping into personal investments, retirement accounts, or home equity, if feasible and appropriate.

2. **Friends and Family:**

- Seek financial support from friends, family members, or personal contacts who believe in the business concept.

- Clearly communicate the terms of the investment and the associated risks to maintain transparency and trust.

3. **Angel Investors:**

- Angel investors are affluent individuals who provide capital to startups in exchange for equity or convertible debt.

- Networking, attending industry events, and working with professional networks can help connect with potential angel investors.

4. **Venture Capital:**

- Venture capital firms provide funding to startups in exchange for equity and often invest large sums of money compared to angel investors.

- It's important to prepare a compelling business plan and pitch to attract venture capital funding.

5. **Small Business Loans:**

- Explore loan options offered by banks, credit unions, or government-backed small business administration (SBA) loans.
- Prepare a comprehensive business plan, financial projections, and collateral, if required, to support the loan application.

6. **Crowdfunding:**
- Utilize online crowdfunding platforms to raise funds from a large number of individuals, often in exchange for rewards, equity, or pre-purchase of products.
- Engage in targeted marketing and promotion to reach potential backers and build momentum for the crowdfunding campaign.

7. **Accelerators and Incubators:**
- Consider participating in startup accelerators and incubator programs that offer funding, mentorship, and resources in exchange for equity.
- Research and apply to reputable accelerator and incubator programs tailored to the specific industry or business focus.

8. **Grants and Competitions:**
- Explore grant opportunities offered by government agencies, non-profit organizations, and private foundations that support entrepreneurial endeavors.
- Participate in business plan competitions and pitch events that offer cash prizes and networking opportunities.

Here is a list of grants:

There are various grants available to support businesses across different industries and at different stages of development. Keep in mind that the availability of grants can change over time, so it's essential to conduct thorough research and verify the current status and eligibility criteria for each grant. Here's a list of potential grants for businesses:

1. **Small Business Innovation Research (SBIR) and Small Business Technology Transfer (STTR) Grants:**
   - These federal programs provide funding for small businesses engaged in research and development with the potential for commercialization.

2. **Small Business Administration (SBA) Grants:**
   - The SBA offers various grant programs and resources to support small businesses, including the Small Business Development Centers (SBDCs) and Women's Business Centers (WBCs).

3. **Economic Development Administration (EDA) Grants:**
   - EDA grants support economic development initiatives, including infrastructure improvements and business development projects in designated regions.

4. **National Institutes of Health (NIH) Grants:**
   - The NIH offers Small Business Innovation Research (SBIR) and Small Business Technology Transfer (STTR) grants to support research and development in the life sciences and healthcare sectors.

5. **Department of Agriculture (USDA) Grants:**
   - The USDA provides grants for rural businesses, agricultural projects, and value-added agricultural initiatives.

6. **National Science Foundation (NSF) Grants:**
   - The NSF offers grants to support innovative research and technology development with commercialization potential.

7. **Environmental Protection Agency (EPA) Grants:**
   - The EPA provides grants to support environmental innovation, pollution reduction, and sustainable business practices.

8. **State and Local Grants:**
   - Many states and local governments offer grants to support small businesses, economic development, and specific industry sectors. These grants may vary widely based on location and economic priorities.

9. **Corporate and Foundation Grants:**

- Some corporations and private foundations offer grants to support small businesses, particularly in areas such as entrepreneurship, technology innovation, and community development.

10. **Research and Development (R&D) Grants:**
   - Various industry-specific organizations and government agencies offer grants to support research and development initiatives, particularly in fields such as advanced manufacturing, clean energy, and technology innovation.

It's important to note that the application processes for grants can be highly competitive and often require detailed proposals, comprehensive business plans, and a clear demonstration of how the grant funds will be used to achieve specific goals. Additionally, eligibility criteria, deadlines, and application requirements can vary significantly among different grant programs. Therefore, entrepreneurs should carefully review the specific details of each grant opportunity and tailor their applications to align with the program's objectives and criteria.

Moreover, entrepreneurs may benefit from seeking guidance from grant-writing resources, consulting with small business development organizations, and leveraging professional networks to increase their chances of successfully securing grants to support their business initiatives.

When seeking funding for a startup, it's essential to meticulously prepare a compelling business plan, financial projections, and a polished pitch that clearly conveys the business concept, market opportunity, and growth potential. Additionally, entrepreneurs should conduct thorough research to identify the most suitable funding sources based on the unique needs and industry of the business. Building relationships with potential investors, demonstrating a strong understanding of the market and competitive landscape, and illustrating a clear path to profitability are critical components of attracting funding for a startup. Moreover, maintaining open communication, transparency, and a clear vision for the business can instill confidence in potential investors and facilitate successful fundraising efforts.

Understanding the Importance of Financial Projections and Cash Flow Management:
Financial projections serve as a roadmap, guiding the business through expected revenues, expenses, and anticipated growth over a defined period. By conducting thorough market and financial analysis, entrepreneurs can craft realistic projections that reflect the business's revenue streams, cost structures, and potential profitability. This insight aids in making informed strategic decisions, securing financing, and forecasting potential cash flow challenges. Cash flow management, on the other hand, focuses on optimizing the inflow and outflow of funds to ensure

the business can meet its financial obligations and maintain liquidity. Employing strategies such as monitoring receivables, managing payables, and contingency planning for lean periods is critical for sustaining the business's financial health.

In conclusion, financial management and budgeting are integral components of business operations, underpinning the fiscal well-being and sustainability of the enterprise. By establishing robust financial systems, developing realistic budgets, encompassing startup costs, and comprehending the significance of financial projections and cash flow management, entrepreneurs can effectively navigate the financial complexities of entrepreneurship. This disciplined approach to financial management not only instills confidence in stakeholders but also equips businesses with the tools and insights necessary to thrive in a competitive economic landscape.

Chapter 5: Building Business Credit

"It's not about ideas. It's about making ideas happen." - Scott Belsky

Understanding Business Credit and Its Importance:
Business credit refers to a business entity's creditworthiness, distinct from the personal credit of its owners. Establishing and maintaining strong business credit is crucial for accessing financing, negotiating favorable terms with vendors and suppliers, and demonstrating financial stability to potential partners and investors. As such, building a robust business credit profile is instrumental for the growth and prosperity of any enterprise, empowering it to access the financial resources required to fuel expansion and navigate through lean periods.

Factors Contributing to a Business Credit Score:
Several key factors contribute to a business's credit score, which serves as a measure of its creditworthiness in the eyes of creditors, lenders, and other business partners. These factors typically

include the business's payment history, credit utilization, length of credit history, new credit accounts, and the types of credit utilized. Prompt and consistent payment of bills and debts, responsible utilization of available credit, and a demonstrated history of managing credit responsibly, all play critical roles in shaping a business's credit score. Understanding these factors empowers business owners to make informed decisions that positively impact their credit standing.

Strategies for Building and Improving Business Credit from Scratch:
Building business credit from the ground up demands strategic planning and deliberate actions to establish a positive credit history. Here are several strategies to consider for those seeking to build and improve their business credit:

- **Establish Separate Business Accounts:** Differentiating personal and business finances is essential. Opening dedicated business bank accounts, obtaining a federal Employer Identification Number (EIN), and incorporating the business as a separate legal entity are important steps in establishing distinct business credit.

- **Obtain Trade Credit and Vendor Accounts:** Initial credit-building activities can involve securing trade credit or vendor accounts with suppliers who report payment histories to business credit bureaus. Timely payments on these accounts can contribute to the positive establishment of the business's credit profile.

- **Apply for a Business Credit Card:** Acquiring a business credit card and utilizing it responsibly can significantly contribute to the development of a positive credit history. Timely payments and prudent management of credit card balances can bolster the business's credit standing.

- **Monitor and Review Business Credit Reports:** Regularly reviewing business credit reports from major credit bureaus enables entrepreneurs to track their credit progress, identify any errors or inaccuracies, and address any issues that may impact their creditworthiness.

- **Cultivate Positive Payment History:** Consistently making on-time payments to creditors and vendors is a cornerstone of building business credit. This demonstrates reliability and fiscal responsibility, laying a strong foundation for a positive credit history.

- **Mindful Credit Utilization:** Prudent utilization of available credit is crucial.

Avoiding maxing out credit lines and maintaining low credit utilization ratios can positively influence the business's credit score.

- **Establish Financial Stability and Credibility:** Demonstrating consistent revenue, profitability, and sound financial management practices can further bolster the business's credibility and creditworthiness in the eyes of creditors and potential partners.

What are the exact steps for building business credit:
Building business credit is an important aspect of establishing a strong financial foundation for your company. Good business credit can help you secure financing, negotiate favorable terms with suppliers, and demonstrate financial stability to potential partners and investors. Here are the steps to building business credit:

- **Establish Your Business Entity**: Ensure that your business is properly registered as a separate legal entity, such as a corporation or LLC. This separation between your personal and business finances is crucial for building distinct business credit.

- **Obtain an EIN:** Apply for an Employer Identification Number (EIN) from the Internal Revenue Service (IRS). This unique identifier for your business is similar to a social security number for individuals and is used for tax purposes and when applying for business credit.

- **Open a Business Bank Account**: Open a dedicated business bank account in the name of your company. This will help separate your personal and business finances and establish a clear track record of business transactions.

- **Obtain a D-U-N-S Number**: Register for a D-U-N-S number from Dun & Bradstreet, a widely used business credit bureau. This unique identifier for your business is used by lenders and suppliers to assess your creditworthiness.

- **Establish Trade Lines:** Work with suppliers and vendors who report payments to business credit bureaus. By establishing trade lines with these entities and consistently making on-time payments, you can build a positive credit history for your business.

- **Apply for a Business Credit Card:** Obtain a business credit card and use it responsibly. Make timely payments and keep your credit utilization low to demonstrate your business's creditworthiness.

- **Monitor Your Credit Report:** Regularly monitor your business credit report from major business credit bureaus such as Dun & Bradstreet, Experian, and Equifax. Ensure that the information is accurate and up to date.

- **Apply for Small Business Loans or Lines of Credit**: As your business credit history strengthens, consider applying for small business loans or lines of credit from financial institutions that report to business credit bureaus. Make timely payments on these accounts to further enhance your credit profile.

- **Pay Bills on Time**: Timely payment of bills, invoices, and credit accounts is crucial for building positive business credit. Late or missed payments can significantly impact your business credit score.

- **Maintain Positive Relationships with Suppliers:** Cultivate positive relationships with your suppliers and consistently fulfill your payment obligations. This can lead to favorable credit terms and references that can bolster your business credit profile.

- **Review and Improve Your Credit Profile:** Continuously evaluate your business credit profile and take steps to address any negative factors. This may include resolving any inaccuracies, managing outstanding debt, and demonstrating responsible financial management.

By following these steps, you can diligently build and maintain a strong business credit profile, which can be instrumental in securing financing, establishing favorable supplier relationships, and showcasing your business's financial reliability and credibility.

Your foolproof plan to obtaining thousands in business credit:

Step 1: Establish the Business Entity and Obtain an EIN
- Register your business as a separate legal entity, such as an LLC or corporation, to create a clear separation between personal and business finances.
- Obtain an Employer Identification Number (EIN) from the IRS, which serves as a unique identifier for your business.

Step 2: Open a Business Bank Account

- Open a dedicated business bank account to differentiate business finances from personal funds. This is crucial for building a clear financial track record.

Step 3: Obtain a D-U-N-S Number
- Register for a D-U-N-S number from Dun & Bradstreet. This identifier is used by creditors and suppliers to assess your business creditworthiness.

Step 4: Establish Trade Lines
- Work with suppliers and vendors who report payments to business credit bureaus. Establish trade lines and consistently make on-time payments to build positive credit history. Starting with Net 30 accounts such as Uline, Grainger, or Quill.

Step 5: Apply for a Business Credit Card
- Apply for a business credit card and use it responsibly. Make timely payments and maintain a low credit utilization ratio to demonstrate creditworthiness.

Step 6: Monitor and Review Your Credit Report
- Regularly monitor your business credit report from major credit bureaus such as Dun & Bradstreet, Experian, and Equifax to ensure accuracy and up-to-date information.

Step 7: Apply for Small Business Loans or Lines of Credit

- As your business credit history strengthens, consider applying for small business loans or lines of credit from institutions that report to business credit bureaus. Make timely payments and manage these accounts responsibly.

Step 8: Pay Bills on Time
- Timely payment of bills, invoices, and credit accounts is crucial for building positive business credit. This demonstrates reliability and creditworthiness.

Step 9: Cultivate Positive Relationships with Suppliers
- Build and maintain positive relationships with suppliers by fulfilling payment obligations promptly. This can lead to favorable credit terms and references that enhance your business credit profile.

Step 10: Review and Improve Your Credit Profile
- Continuously assess your business credit profile and take steps to address any negative factors. This may involve resolving inaccuracies, managing outstanding debt, and demonstrating responsible financial management.

Step 11: Establish a Strong Financial Track Record
- Build a strong financial track record by maintaining positive cash flow, managing debt effectively, and consistently meeting financial obligations.

Step 12: Maintain Consistent Financial Health
- Continue to manage your business's finances prudently, as responsible financial management is essential for maintaining and improving your business credit.

By following this plan, you can systematically build and maintain a strong business credit profile, which is crucial for securing financing, establishing favorable supplier relationships, and showcasing your business's financial reliability and credibility.

Tiered business credit accounts:
Tiered business credit accounts refer to lines of credit or financing options that are structured into different tiers or levels based on the creditworthiness and financial stability of a business. These tiers typically offer varying levels of credit limits, interest rates, and terms, providing businesses with options that align with their credit profile and financial needs.

In this context, tiered business credit accounts can be offered by financial institutions, such as banks or credit unions, or through business credit card issuers. The tiers are often determined based on the business's credit history, revenue, length of time in business, and other financial factors.

Here are some common features of tiered business credit accounts:

- **Tiered Credit Limits:** Businesses with stronger credit profiles and financial stability may be eligible for higher credit limits, while those with limited credit history or lower financial standing may start with lower credit limits. As the business demonstrates responsible credit usage and improves its financial health, it may become eligible for higher-tier credit limits.

- **Varied Interest Rates:** Different tiers may be associated with varying interest rates. Businesses in higher tiers with stronger credit profiles may receive lower interest rates, while those in lower tiers with more risk may face higher rates. This structure allows businesses to access credit at rates that reflect their risk level and creditworthiness.

- **Diverse Terms and Benefits:** Tiered business credit accounts may offer different terms, rewards, and benefits based on the tier. For example, businesses in higher tiers may receive perks such as cash back rewards, travel benefits, or access to premium services, while lower-tier accounts may have more basic features.

- **Path to Advancement:** Businesses in lower tiers may have the opportunity to improve their credit profile and qualify for higher tiers over time. By responsibly managing their credit accounts and demonstrating financial stability, businesses can work towards advancing to more favorable tiers with increased credit limits and better terms.

It's important for businesses to understand the structure and terms of tiered business credit accounts when evaluating their financing options. By choosing the right tier based on their creditworthiness and financial needs, businesses can access the appropriate level of financing while working to improve their credit standing over time.

Additionally, businesses should carefully review the terms and conditions of tiered business credit accounts, including fees, penalties, and repayment structures, to ensure that they align with their financial goals and capabilities.

Overall, tiered business credit accounts provide businesses with flexibility and the potential for growth as they establish and build their credit profiles, making them a valuable tool for managing cash flow, making purchases, and investing in business growth.

In the context of business credit accounts, the terms "Tier 1," "Tier 2," and "Tier 3" generally refer to different levels or tiers of creditworthiness and financial stability that businesses may fall into when seeking financing. These tiers are typically used by financial institutions and credit card issuers to classify businesses based on their credit profiles, and each tier may offer varying credit limits, interest rates, and benefits.

Here's a general overview of how these tiers are commonly structured:

Tier 1:
- Tier 1 typically represents the highest level of creditworthiness for businesses. Businesses in Tier 1 often have strong credit profiles, a demonstrated history of responsible credit management, and solid financial stability.
- Features of Tier 1 credit accounts may include higher credit limits, lower interest rates, and access to additional perks, rewards, and premium services.
- Businesses in Tier 1 are generally considered lower risk by lenders and may receive the most favorable terms and conditions for credit accounts.

Tier 2:
- Tier 2 represents a middle level of creditworthiness, falling between Tier 1 and Tier 3. Businesses in Tier 2 may have good credit profiles and financial stability, but they might not meet all the criteria for Tier 1.
- Credit accounts in Tier 2 may offer moderate credit limits and somewhat competitive interest rates. The benefits and features associated with

Tier 2 accounts generally fall between those of Tier 1 and Tier 3.

Tier 3:
- Tier 3 typically represents the lowest level of creditworthiness among the tiers. Businesses in Tier 3 may have more limited credit histories, lower financial stability, or higher perceived risk from the perspective of lenders.
- Credit accounts in Tier 3 may offer lower credit limits, higher interest rates, and fewer additional benefits compared to higher tiers. Businesses in Tier 3 may still be eligible for credit, but they may face more stringent terms and conditions.

It's important to note that the specific criteria for classifying businesses into these tiers can vary between financial institutions and credit card issuers. Factors such as credit scores, payment history, business revenue, length of time in operation, and other financial indicators are often used to determine which tier a business falls into.

When businesses are classified into these tiers, it helps lenders and credit issuers to assess risk and offer financing options that are tailored to the creditworthiness and financial standing of each business. Understanding these tiers can assist businesses in selecting the most suitable credit accounts based on their financial situation and in working towards improving their credit standing to

access more favorable financing options in the
future.

It's important for businesses to regularly monitor
their credit profiles, manage their credit responsibly,
and seek opportunities to strengthen their financial
health, as this can ultimately help them qualify for
more favorable credit terms and potentially move
into higher tiers of creditworthiness.

In conclusion, building and maintaining strong
business credit is a critical component of
establishing a solid financial foundation and
facilitating the growth and success of any
enterprise. Understanding the concept of business
credit, recognizing the factors that influence credit
scores, and implementing strategic measures to
build and improve business credit from scratch
empowers entrepreneurs to effectively leverage
financial resources and establish credibility within
the business community. By employing these
strategies with diligence and discipline,
entrepreneurs can position their businesses for
long-term financial health and prosperity.

Chapter 6: Establishing a Strong Business Presence

"The best way to predict the future is to create it." - Peter Drucker

Creating a professional website, establishing a business phone number, and securing a business address are critical steps for establishing an online presence and maintaining accessibility for your business. Here's a comprehensive guide on how to accomplish these tasks:

1. **Creating a Professional Website:**
   a. Choose a Domain Name: Select a domain name that reflects your business name or describes your products/services. Use domain registration services to check availability and secure your chosen domain.
   b. **Select a Web Hosting Service:** Research web hosting providers to find a service that meets your needs in terms of storage, bandwidth, uptime, and customer support.
   c. **Design and Development:** Create your website using a website builder, content management system (CMS), or by hiring a web developer if needed. Ensure that your website design is visually appealing, user-friendly, and optimized for both desktop and mobile devices.

d. **Content Creation:** Develop high-quality content, including engaging copy, images, videos, and other media that effectively showcases your business offerings and brand identity.

e. **Search Engine Optimization (SEO):** Implement SEO best practices to improve your website's visibility on search engines and attract organic traffic. This includes optimizing page titles, meta descriptions, keywords, and creating valuable content.

f. **Security and Compliance:** Ensure that your website is secure by using SSL certificates, implementing data protection measures, and adhering to relevant privacy regulations such as GDPR or CCPA.

g. **Launch and Maintenance:** Once your website is ready, launch it and regularly update its content, monitor performance, and address any technical issues that may arise.

2. **Establishing a Business Phone Number:**

a. **Choose a Phone Service Provider:** Research phone service providers offering business phone solutions, such as traditional landlines, Voice over Internet Protocol (VoIP), or virtual phone systems. Consider features such as call forwarding, voicemail, and auto-attendant.

b. **Select the Number:** Decide whether to get a toll-free number, a local number, or a vanity number that is easy to remember.

c. **Setup and Configuration:** Follow the provider's instructions to set up your business phone number, configure call routing, voicemail greetings, and other features based on your business needs.

d. **Integration:** Integrate your business phone system with customer relationship management (CRM) software, helpdesk solutions, and other tools to streamline communication and customer support processes.

Download and pay for the Grasshopper App to receive an alternative phone number that will be linked to your cell phone.

3. **Securing a Business Address:**

a. **Virtual Office or Coworking Space:** Consider renting a virtual office address or utilizing a coworking space that provides a professional business address for mail and package delivery.

b. **P.O. Box or Mailbox Service:** Rent a P.O. Box at a local post office or a private mailbox service that offers a street address for business correspondence.

c. **Commercial Office Space:** If your business requires a physical location for operations, lease or purchase commercial office space that aligns with your budget and business requirements.

Remember that when establishing a business website and contact information, it's crucial to maintain consistent branding across all platforms, provide accurate and updated information, and ensure compliance with relevant regulations, such as data protection laws and local business requirements. By effectively executing these steps, you can create a professional and accessible online presence for your business, facilitating customer engagement and trust.

Creating a Professional Brand Identity and Online Presence:
In the digital era, a strong and professional brand identity is essential for capturing the attention of potential customers and standing out in a competitive market. Crafting a compelling brand identity involves defining the business's mission, values, and unique selling proposition, and translating these elements into a cohesive visual representation through a distinctive logo, color scheme, and visual assets. This brand identity should be consistently reflected across all communication channels, from websites and social media profiles to physical promotional materials, conveying a sense of professionalism, credibility, and reliability to the target audience.

Building an effective online presence is equally crucial. An engaging, user-friendly website that reflects the brand's identity and offers valuable content, such as product information, educational resources, and customer testimonials, serves as a powerful digital storefront. It not only facilitates customer engagement but also establishes the business as a credible and authoritative resource within its industry.

**Using Effective Marketing and Networking
Strategies to Attract Customers:**
Effective marketing and networking strategies are
essential for attracting and retaining customers.
Leveraging digital marketing techniques, such as
search engine optimization (SEO), content
marketing, email campaigns, and pay-per-click
advertising, allows businesses to reach their target
audience with precision and relevance. Well-crafted
marketing materials, including brochures, flyers,
and business cards, can also serve as valuable
tools for offline promotion and networking.

Networking with other businesses, industry
influencers, and potential customers through
events, trade shows, and professional
organizations presents valuable opportunities to
build strategic partnerships and generate leads.
Effective networking entails active engagement,
genuine relationship-building, and a willingness to
offer value to others in the business ecosystem.

**Leveraging Social Media and Other Platforms to
Promote the Business:**
Social media platforms offer powerful tools for
promoting businesses and engaging with
customers. Establishing a strong presence on
platforms relevant to the business's target
audience, such as Facebook, Instagram, LinkedIn,
and Twitter, allows for direct interaction with
customers, dissemination of engaging content, and
amplification of brand messaging. It also provides a

platform for showcasing products or services, sharing customer testimonials, and humanizing the brand through behind-the-scenes glimpses and employee spotlights.

Leveraging social media advertising further amplifies the reach of promotional content and enables precise targeting based on demographics, interests, and behaviors. Consistent, authentic engagement with followers, timely responses to queries and concerns, and the cultivation of a community around the brand contribute to a positive brand image and customer loyalty.

Beyond social media, platforms such as industry-specific forums, review sites, and online marketplaces provide additional avenues for promoting the business and engaging with potential customers. Leveraging these platforms effectively involves monitoring and responding to customer feedback, actively participating in relevant discussions, and harnessing these channels as additional touchpoints to enhance the overall customer experience.

In summary, establishing a strong business presence necessitates the crafting of a compelling brand identity, developing a robust online presence, and employing effective marketing and networking strategies to attract and retain customers. By focusing on creating a professional brand image, engaging with the target audience through relevant marketing and networking channels, and leveraging social media and other digital platforms to promote the business, entrepreneurs can effectively position their ventures for visibility, credibility, and sustained growth in today's competitive business landscape.

Chapter 7: Legal and Regulatory Considerations

"The only place where success comes before work is in the dictionary." - Vidal Sassoon

Navigating the Legal and Regulatory Requirements for Starting a Business:
Starting a business involves navigating a complex web of legal and regulatory requirements, which can vary based on the business's location, industry, and structure. Understanding the legal framework and compliance obligations is essential for ensuring that the business operates within the boundaries of the law from its inception. This includes choosing the appropriate business structure, such as sole proprietorship, partnership, limited liability company (LLC), or corporation, and fulfilling the associated legal formalities and documentation.

Furthermore, adherence to industry-specific regulations, zoning laws, and environmental standards is crucial for avoiding potential legal issues and maintaining ethical business practices. Incorporating legal considerations into the early stages of business planning can help mitigate legal risks, establish a compliant operational framework, and foster a culture of accountability and responsibility within the organization.

Understanding Tax Obligations, Licenses, Permits, and Other Legal Considerations:
Entrepreneurs must familiarize themselves with tax obligations at the federal, state, and local levels, as well as the associated filing requirements and deadlines. This includes understanding income tax, sales tax, employment tax, and other tax liabilities relevant to the business's operations. Additionally, obtaining the necessary licenses and permits, such as business licenses, health permits, and professional certifications, is vital for legal operation and to avoid potential penalties or business interruptions.

Intellectual property considerations, including trademarks, copyrights, and patents, are also essential for protecting the business's unique assets and ideas. Understanding the legal mechanisms for intellectual property protection can safeguard the business from infringement and unauthorized use of its intellectual assets.

Protecting the Business Through Appropriate Insurance and Risk Management:
Risk management is an integral aspect of legal and regulatory compliance. Entrepreneurs should assess potential risks inherent to their business activities and implement strategies to mitigate and

transfer these risks. This may involve obtaining suitable business insurance coverage, including general liability insurance, professional liability insurance, property insurance, and workers' compensation insurance, to protect against unforeseen liabilities, damages, and legal claims.

Compliance with workplace safety regulations and the implementation of robust internal control measures are crucial for preserving the well-being of employees and the business's operational continuity. By integrating risk management practices into the business's operational framework, entrepreneurs can safeguard against potential legal disputes, financial losses, and reputational damage.

Explain tax obligations of different business structures:
The tax obligations for different business structures can vary significantly. Here's an overview of the tax considerations for common business entities:

1. **Sole Proprietorship:**
   - **Tax Filing:** As a sole proprietor, you report business income and expenses on your personal tax return using Schedule C (Form 1040) along with your regular Form 1040.
   - **Self-Employment Taxes:** Sole proprietors are responsible for paying self-employment taxes, which cover Social Security and Medicare taxes based on their business's net earnings.

- **Estimated Taxes:** Sole proprietors are typically required to make quarterly estimated tax payments to cover income tax and self-employment tax liabilities.

2. **Partnership:**
- **Pass-Through Taxation:** Partnerships are pass-through entities, which means the business itself does not pay income taxes. Instead, the profits and losses pass through to the partners, who report their share on their individual tax returns.
- **Form 1065:** The partnership must file an informational return (Form 1065) to report its income, deductions, credits, and other tax-related items. The partnership issues Schedule K-1 to each partner, detailing their share of the partnership's income, losses, deductions, and credits.

3. **Limited Liability Company (LLC):**
- **Flexibility:** LLCs have flexibility in choosing their tax treatment. They can be taxed as a sole proprietorship, partnership (if multiple members), S corporation, or C corporation.
- **Default Classification:** By default, a single-member LLC is treated as a disregarded entity for tax purposes, similar to a sole proprietorship. Multi-member LLCs are treated as partnerships unless they elect otherwise.
- **Option for S Corporation Status:** LLCs can elect to be taxed as an S corporation, allowing for pass-through taxation while potentially reducing

self-employment tax burden, although certain requirements must be met.

4. **C Corporation:**

   - **Double Taxation:** C corporations are taxed as separate legal entities, and they file a corporate tax return (Form 1120). The corporation pays taxes on its profits, and if dividends are distributed to shareholders, those dividends are taxed again on the shareholders' individual tax returns.

   - **Corporate Tax Rates:** C corporations are subject to corporate income tax rates, which are distinct from individual income tax rates. The tax rates for C corporations are based on the corporation's taxable income.

5. **S Corporation:**

   - **Pass-Through Taxation:** S corporations are pass-through entities, meaning they do not pay federal income tax at the corporate level. Instead, profits and losses are passed through to shareholders, who report them on their individual tax returns.

   - **Form 1120S:** S corporations file an informational tax return (Form 1120S) to report income, deductions, credits, and other tax-related items. The corporation issues Schedule K-1 to each shareholder, detailing their share of the corporation's income, losses, deductions, and credits.

It's important to note that tax obligations for businesses may be subject to specific state and local tax requirements in addition to federal tax laws. It's advisable for business owners to consult with tax advisors or certified public accountants to understand the intricacies of tax planning, ensure compliance with tax laws, and optimize their tax strategies based on their specific business structure and financial circumstances.

In summary, tackling the legal and regulatory considerations of starting and operating a business entails navigating compliance requirements, understanding tax obligations, licenses, permits, intellectual property protection, and implementing risk management strategies. By proactively addressing these legal and regulatory aspects, entrepreneurs can establish a solid legal foundation, fulfill their obligations, and protect their businesses from potential legal entanglements and financial liabilities.

Chapter 8: Securing Funding and Financing Options

"The entrepreneur always searches for change, responds to it, and exploits it as an opportunity." - Peter Drucker

Exploring Different Sources of Business Funding:

Securing adequate funding is a critical step in launching and sustaining a new business. Entrepreneurs have various options when seeking financial resources, including traditional bank loans, venture capital investments, angel investors, personal savings, crowdfunding, and government grants. Each funding source comes with its distinct terms, conditions, and implications, and it is essential for entrepreneurs to understand the nuances of each option to make informed decisions aligned with their business goals and financial needs.

Understanding the Pros and Cons of Each Funding Option:

Different funding sources offer unique advantages and drawbacks. Traditional bank loans may provide reliable capital but often require collateral and have stringent borrowing criteria. Venture capital and angel investors can inject substantial funds into a business but typically involve giving up equity and relinquishing some control. Crowdfunding platforms offer a way to raise capital from a broad base of supporters, but success is not guaranteed, and it requires a significant marketing effort.

Personal savings provide autonomy and control but can limit the entrepreneur's financial security. Government grants offer non-repayable funding but often come with strict eligibility criteria and compliance requirements. It is essential for entrepreneurs to weigh these pros and cons, considering factors such as cost of capital, ownership dilution, repayment obligations, and the potential impact on long-term business sustainability.

Tips for Securing Financing for a New Business and Managing Financial Resources Effectively: Securing financing for a new business requires thorough preparation, strategic planning, and effective communication. Entrepreneurs can enhance their chances of securing funding by developing a comprehensive business plan, a robust financial forecast, and a compelling value proposition for potential investors or lenders. Demonstrating a clear understanding of the market, competitive landscape, and the capability to execute the business strategy is vital for building confidence in the business's potential for success.

Managing financial resources effectively involves prudent cash flow management, rigorous budgeting, and disciplined use of funds. Entrepreneurs should prioritize allocating capital to essential operational needs, monitoring and controlling expenses, and seeking cost-effective solutions to optimize financial resources. Establishing strong financial management practices, including accurate record-keeping, financial transparency, and timely financial reporting, helps build credibility with stakeholders and supports sustainable business growth.

Moreover, entrepreneurs should continuously evaluate the business's financial performance, adapt to changing market conditions, and proactively seek out potential funding sources and opportunities. Developing strong relationships with financial institutions, investors, and potential funding partners can provide access to valuable financial resources and advisory support.

In conclusion, securing funding and financing options for a new business requires a comprehensive understanding of different funding sources, their pros and cons, and the ability to effectively communicate the business's potential to investors and lenders. By aligning the funding strategy with the business's long-term objectives and implementing prudent financial management practices, entrepreneurs can increase the likelihood of securing the necessary capital and effectively managing financial resources to support the business's growth and sustainability.

Marketing for your Business:
A winning marketing strategy for your business is essential to attract and retain customers, build brand awareness, and drive growth. Here are key components to consider when developing a comprehensive marketing strategy:

- **Target Audience Identification:** Clearly define your target audience based on factors such as demographics, behaviors, and preferences. Understand their needs, pain points, and aspirations to tailor your marketing efforts effectively.

- **Unique Selling Proposition (USP):** Identify and articulate what sets your business apart from competitors. Communicate your USP clearly through your marketing materials to resonate with your target audience.

- **Branding and Positioning:** Develop a strong brand identity that reflects your values, mission, and personality. Ensure consistency across all marketing channels to create a cohesive brand image.

- **Multi-Channel Marketing:** Utilize a mix of digital and traditional marketing channels to reach your audience. This may include social media, content marketing, email campaigns, search engine optimization (SEO), pay-per-click (PPC) advertising, influencer partnerships, and offline tactics like events and print media.

- **Content Creation:** Develop high-quality, relevant content that educates, entertains, or inspires your audience. This could include blog posts, videos, infographics, webinars, and podcasts.

- **Customer Relationship Management (CRM):** Implement strategies to engage and build relationships with your customers. This may involve personalized communication, loyalty programs, feedback mechanisms, and exceptional customer service.

- **Data-Driven Approach:** Leverage data analytics to understand customer behavior, track the performance of marketing campaigns, and make informed decisions to optimize your strategy.

- **Conversion Optimization:** Focus on converting leads into customers by optimizing your website, landing pages, and sales funnels. A/B testing and user experience improvements can help maximize conversion rates.

- **Community Engagement:** Foster a community around your brand by engaging with customers on social media, hosting events, or supporting causes aligned with your brand values.

- **Continuous Refinement:** Regularly review and refine your marketing strategy based on performance metrics, industry trends, and customer feedback.

Remember that a winning marketing strategy is not set in stone and should continuously evolve to adapt to market dynamics and customer preferences. It's also important to track the return on investment (ROI) of your marketing efforts to ensure that you are efficiently allocating resources to the most effective channels and activities. By incorporating these elements into your marketing strategy, you can create a compelling and sustainable plan to drive the success of your business.

Chapter 9: Managing Growth and Scaling the Business

"Your most unhappy customers are your greatest source of learning." - Bill Gates

Strategies for Scaling the Business While Maintaining Financial Stability:
Scaling a business involves expanding its operations, customer base, and market presence while ensuring sustainable growth and maintaining financial stability. Entrepreneurs can employ several strategies to effectively scale their businesses, such as implementing efficient operational processes, leveraging technology and automation, expanding product lines or service offerings, and entering new markets. It is essential to strike a balance between growth and financial stability by carefully managing cash flow, optimizing resource allocation, and forecasting financial needs accurately.

Managing Expansion, Hiring Employees, and Building a Strong Team:
As a business expands, hiring employees and building a strong team become pivotal to supporting growth and delivering exceptional products or services. Entrepreneurs should focus on strategic workforce planning, hiring talented individuals who

align with the company's culture and vision, and investing in employee development and retention strategies. Building a strong organizational structure, fostering a collaborative work environment, and empowering employees with the right tools and resources are essential for successful business scaling.

Understanding the Challenges and Opportunities of Business Growth:
Business growth presents both challenges and opportunities that entrepreneurs must navigate effectively. Challenges may include managing increased operational complexity, maintaining consistent product or service quality, and adapting to changes in customer demands and market dynamics. Opportunities may arise in the form of accessing new markets, forming strategic partnerships, and leveraging economies of scale to drive profitability. It is crucial for entrepreneurs to anticipate potential challenges, proactively address them, and capitalize on opportunities to sustainably scale their businesses.

Furthermore, addressing scalability issues related to supply chain management, production capacity, and infrastructure is critical to support business growth. Implementing scalable technology solutions and processes and continually refining operational efficiency are essential for managing the complexities of expansion.

In conclusion, managing growth and scaling a business requires a strategic approach that balances expansion and financial stability. By implementing effective scaling strategies, nurturing a strong workforce, and addressing the challenges and opportunities that come with growth, entrepreneurs can set their businesses on a path for sustainable expansion and long-term success.

Chapter 10: Navigating Pitfalls and Ensuring Long-Term Success

"In the modern world of business, it is useless to be a creative, original thinker unless you can also sell what you create." - David Ogilvy

Identifying Common Pitfalls and Challenges Faced by New Business Owners:
Starting a new business comes with its set of challenges and pitfalls that entrepreneurs must navigate to ensure long-term success. Common hurdles include financial constraints, market competition, operational inefficiencies, and unforeseen regulatory or legal issues. Additionally, managing rapid growth, maintaining customer satisfaction, and adapting to industry disruptions are critical challenges that new business owners often encounter. It is essential for entrepreneurs to proactively identify these potential pitfalls and develop strategies to address them effectively.

Tips for Overcoming Obstacles and Adapting to Changes in the Business Landscape:
To overcome obstacles and adapt to changes in the business landscape, entrepreneurs should prioritize resilience, flexibility, and continuous learning. Embracing innovation, seeking mentorship, and leveraging technological advancements can help

businesses adapt to evolving market trends. Furthermore, fostering a culture of agility, empowering employees to contribute to problem-solving, and maintaining open lines of communication with customers and stakeholders are essential practices for overcoming obstacles and adapting to change. Additionally, building a resilient financial strategy, maintaining a strong network of support, and staying attuned to industry shifts are essential for navigating challenges and sustaining business success.

Planning for Long-Term Success and Sustainability in the Competitive Business World:

Long-term success and sustainability in the competitive business world require thoughtful planning, strategic foresight, and a commitment to continuous improvement. Entrepreneurs should focus on establishing a clear vision, mission, and core values for their businesses, alongside setting achievable long-term goals. Developing a robust business continuity plan, monitoring key performance indicators, and regularly assessing market dynamics and customer needs are crucial for sustained success. Furthermore, investing in ongoing innovation, talent development, and customer experience enhancement can position businesses for long-term growth and relevance in a dynamic marketplace.

In conclusion, effectively navigating pitfalls and ensuring long-term success in the business world requires a proactive approach to identifying challenges, overcoming obstacles, and planning for sustained growth. By embracing resilience, fostering adaptability, and prioritizing long-term strategic planning, entrepreneurs can position their businesses for enduring success in a competitive and ever-evolving business landscape.

Conclusion:

As we draw the final pages of "The Entrepreneur's Blueprint," it is with the utmost conviction that we affirm the transformative potential inherent in the journey of building a business and mastering business credit. This endeavor is not merely about financial transactions, corporate structures, or credit scores; it is a testament to the enduring spirit of entrepreneurship, vision, and tenacity.

Throughout this book, we have embarked on an immersive exploration of the multifaceted landscape of entrepreneurship, from conceiving innovative business ideas to navigating the labyrinth of financial credibility. We have uncovered the pivotal role of brand identity, market positioning, and strategic marketing in shaping businesses that resonate with audiences and carve a niche in competitive industries.

Delving into the realm of business credit, we have unraveled the nuances of establishing and fortifying a robust credit profile, empowering you to lay the foundation for financial stability, access capital, and cultivate enduring relationships with stakeholders in your business ecosystem.

It is our fervent hope that the insights, strategies, and real-world examples shared within these pages have ignited the flames of creativity, resilience, and strategic acumen within you, equipping you to navigate the challenges and triumphs that await in your entrepreneurial journey.

As the concluding chapter of this book unfolds, we invite you to seize the boundless opportunities that entrepreneurship affords, to transcend limitations, and to endeavor with unwavering resolve. The path ahead may be adorned with trials and uncertainties, yet it is also adorned with the potential for impact, innovation, and transformative success.

In closing, remember that the pursuit of entrepreneurship is a tapestry woven with perseverance, visionary leadership, and an unwavering commitment to excellence. May the knowledge and wisdom gleaned from "The Entrepreneur's Blueprint" propel you toward unparalleled success, enabling you to weave your own narrative of triumph in the entrepreneurial landscape.

Whether you are standing at the precipice of launching your entrepreneurial voyage or seeking to fortify the foundations of an existing business, may the knowledge encapsulated within these pages serve as a torch to illuminate the path forward, a compass to navigate uncharted territories, and a steadfast companion in your pursuit of entrepreneurial excellence.

As you turn the final page of this book, may you carry forth the wisdom, fortitude, and unyielding spirit of innovation, ready to inscribe your unique mark on the world through your entrepreneurial endeavors. The journey of entrepreneurship and financial acumen is a testament to human ingenuity, resilience, and the relentless pursuit of transformative impact. Embrace it with unwavering resolve and empowered confidence.

Go forth and seize the boundless opportunities that await on the horizon, knowing that your business and credit journey is fortified with the wisdom and insights of "The Entrepreneur's Blueprint." Your entrepreneurial odyssey awaits—may it be filled with triumphs, resilience, and enduring success.

Glossary:

Accounts Payable: The amount of money a company owes to its suppliers and vendors for goods or services purchased on credit.

Balance Sheet: A financial statement that provides a snapshot of a company's assets, liabilities, and shareholders' equity at a specific point in time.

Branding: The process of creating a unique and recognizable identity for a business, encompassing its name, logo, visual elements, and messaging to differentiate it from competitors and resonate with customers.

Business Address: The physical location or mailing address of a business entity, often used for official correspondence, registration, and branding purposes.

Business Credit: The credit profile and history of a business entity, used by lenders, suppliers, and other stakeholders to assess its financial reliability and creditworthiness.

Business Credit Card: A credit card issued to a business entity, used to make purchases, manage cash flow, and build a credit history separately from the owner's personal credit.

Business Credit Relationship: The interaction and financial transactions between a business entity and its suppliers, creditors, lenders, and financial partners.

Business Phone Number: A dedicated phone line for a business, enabling communication with customers, suppliers, and stakeholders while maintaining a professional image.

Business Plan: A written document that outlines the goals, objectives, strategies, and financial forecasts of a business, serving as a roadmap for its operations and growth.

Business Structure: The legal framework that defines the ownership, liabilities, and taxation of a business, including options such as sole proprietorship, partnership, limited liability company (LLC), corporation, and cooperative.

Cash Flow: The movement of money into and out of a business, including revenue, expenses, and investments.

Credit Monitoring: The practice of regularly reviewing and assessing a business's credit reports and scores to identify changes, errors, or potential fraud and ensure optimal credit health.

Credit Reporting Agency: An organization that collects and maintains credit information on businesses and individuals, generating credit reports and scores used by lenders and creditors to assess credit risk.

Credit Utilization: The percentage of a business's available credit that is currently being used, impacting its credit score and financial health.

Depreciation: The decrease in the value of an asset over time, reflecting its use, wear and tear, and obsolescence.

EIN (Employer Identification Number): A unique nine-digit number assigned by the Internal Revenue Service (IRS) to identify a business entity for federal tax purposes.

Entrepreneurship: The act of identifying, creating, and pursuing opportunities to build and grow a business, often involving innovation, risk-taking, and strategic vision.

Equity: The ownership interest in a company that represents the residual value of its assets after deducting liabilities.

Financial Stability: The state of a business's financial condition characterized by sustainable revenue, manageable debt, positive cash flow, and the ability to weather economic uncertainties.

Financial Statements: Documents (such as the income statement, balance sheet, and cash flow statement) that present the financial performance and position of a company.

Funding: The financial resources, such as capital, investment, or loans, utilized to start and sustain a business's operations and growth.

Gross Profit: The revenue left after deducting the cost of goods sold from total revenue.

Inventory Turnover: A measure of how many times a company's inventory is sold and replaced over a specific period, indicating efficiency in managing inventory

Liquidity: The ease with which an asset can be converted into cash without affecting its market price, reflecting a company's ability to meet short-term obligations.

Marketing Strategy: The comprehensive plan outlining the tactics and approaches to promote and sell a business's products or services to its target audience, encompassing market research, advertising, and digital marketing.

Small Business Loan: A financial product designed specifically for small businesses, providing capital for various purposes such as startup costs, expansion, equipment purchase, or working capital.

Profit Margin: A ratio that measures a company's profitability, indicating the percentage of profit derived from its revenue.

Trade Lines: The credit accounts, such as loans, credit cards, or lines of credit, reported to credit bureaus and reflected in a business's credit report.

Treasury Stock: Shares of a company's own stock that it has issued and subsequently repurchased, but not retired.

References

7 business scaling strategies for growing your business | upwork. (n.d.). https://www.upwork.com/resources/scaling-a-business

Beers, B. (n.d.). *6 steps to a better business budget*. Investopedia. https://www.investopedia.com/articles/pf/08/small-business-budget.asp#:~:text=Budgeting%20is%20an%20easy%2C%20but,ensure%20a%20solid%20emergency%20fund.

Choose a business structure. U.S. Small Business Administration. (n.d.-a). https://www.sba.gov/business-guide/launch-your-business/choose-business-structure

Dedes, M., Dedes, M., Dedes matt@employeeconnect.com, M., & Matt@employeeconnect.com. (2023, November 29). *Navigating the future: The triad of governance, risk management, and audit in 2023*. EmployeeConnect HRIS. https://www.employeeconnect.com/blog/navigating-the-future-the-triad-of-governance-risk-management-and-audit-in-2023/

Establish Business Credit. U.S. Small Business Administration. (n.d.-b).

https://www.sba.gov/business-guide/plan-you
r-business/establish-business-credit

The five stages of small-business growth.
Harvard Business Review. (2023, June 16).
https://hbr.org/1983/05/the-five-stages-of-sma
ll-business-growth

Fund your business. U.S. Small Business
Administration. (n.d.-c).
https://www.sba.gov/business-guide/plan-you
r-business/fund-your-business#:~:text=To%2
0increase%20your%20chances%20of,by%20
giving%20you%20a%20loan.

Group, U. (2023, February 6). *How to build a
strong online presence for your business.*
Credit Card Processing & Merchant Services
- Unicorn Group.
https://unicorngroup.ch/blog/how-to-build-onli
ne-presence/

Investopedia. (n.d.). *Entrepreneur: What it
means to be one and how to get started.*
Investopedia.
https://www.investopedia.com/terms/e/entrepr
eneur.asp#:~:text=Entrepreneurship%20is%2
0when%20an%20individual,with%20an%20in
novative%20new%20idea.

Small business legal concerns to consider.
Nevada Small Business. (2022, August 17).

https://nevadasmallbusiness.com/small-busin
ess-legal-issues/

team, Aic. (2023, November 6). *Overcoming
entrepreneurship challenges: Strategies for
navigating obstacles and thriving.*
https://aicontentfy.com/en/blog/overcoming-e
ntrepreneurship-challenges-strategies-for-nav
igating-obstacles-and-thriving-1#:~:text=Cons
tantly%20monitor%20and%20analyze%20the
,customer%20service%20and%20personaliz
ed%20experiences.

Write your business plan. U.S. Small
Business Administration. (n.d.-d).
https://www.sba.gov/business-guide/plan-you
r-business/write-your-business-plan

www.ingramcontent.com/pod-product-compliance
Lightning Source LLC
Chambersburg PA
CBHW031319250726
48656CB00005B/1874